ON MORALS

Book Design & Production:
Columbus Publishing Lab
www.ColumbusPublishingLab.com

Copyright © 2022 by
Jack Lutat
LCCN: PENDING

Paperback ISBN: 978-1-63337-613-7

Printed in the United States of America
1 3 5 7 9 10 8 6 4 2

ON MORALS

INVESTIGATING LOYALTY

PHILOSOPHY PRESENTED BY
JACK LUTAT

DEDICATION

This short book is dedicated to all people, in hopes that these words spur self-reflection and encourage deep thought on what we hold dear in our lives. I further dedicate this to the people who do not read this as fact, but remain open-minded to interpret these investigations how they will and enhance the ways in which they interact with friends, family, community, and beyond. Thank you all for cracking open this book and taking a moment read.

On Morals

Philosophy presented by Jack Lutat

I'VE BEEN FASCINATED with this idea of "loyalty" for quite some time. What is it? Where does it take us? Why is it important? When we step back and take a look at our lives, asking ourselves in what ways we are loyal, the immediate thought may conjure images of friends, family, perhaps even some mentors and mentees. Perhaps you think of businesses, maybe brand loyalty, or even duty. Loyalty is a powerful moral idea, and henceforth for this paper, I intend on using morals within my broadly interpretable definition of loyalty: *loyalty is rooted in trust and conducive to survival.* This doesn't describe what loyalty *qua* loyalty is, but perhaps loyalty can be inferred as the movement of trust from one person to another, from the giver of trust to the recipient. Thus, loyalty doesn't quite fit the framework of a *thing* but rather an *action*.

Under this broad interpretation of loyalty, we can cast our trust into a great many things. We might be loyal to a great many people or a great many things. For instance, I'm loyal to this computer which I type on. I'm loyal to it on a material basis. I trust that I can rely on using it for its intended purposes, and it helps me to survive in the socioeconomic climate of our current world. Hence, my loyalty into this object is not misplaced, and is duly founded on my experiences and knowledge of this *thing*. My trust in this object implies that I will return to it, for it accomplishes functions that I cannot complete without it.

Now, I'll posit a diagram that may seem overwhelming, but it illuminates in many ways how loyalty seeps into society, but also illustrates how loyalty births morality on not merely personal scales, but on scales greater than or equal to all of humanity. I separate morals, ethics, and laws and keep humanity and legal systems confined within the realm of ethics and laws respectfully. However, morals, morality, loyalty carry such profound meaning and implicit magnitude throughout the other two afore-mentioned principles that we must analyze how loyalty spawns different values of morality that impact our treatment of others, our interpersonal relationships, and the structures of the sovereignties around the world.

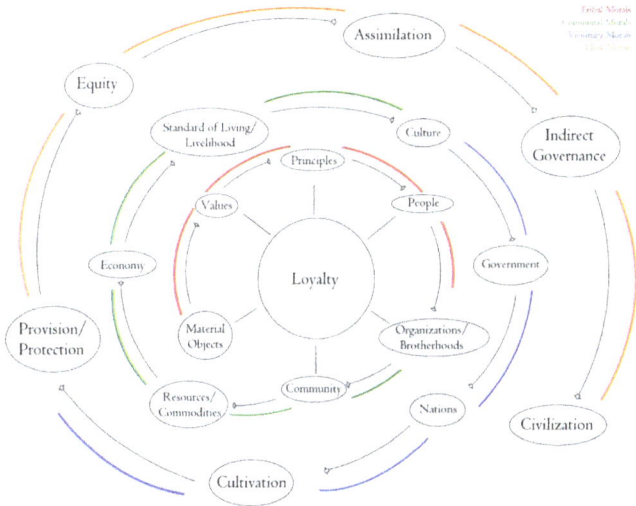

Figure 1: The Spiral of Loyalty

Start in the center and spiral outwards from *Material Objects.* This will show you the natural progression of ever grander ideas. Now, we will begin our discussion from the intended starting point.

TRIBAL MORALS

Material Objects. Material objects can mean any matter you lay your hands on. It could truly be a noun that manifests a physical form. As humans, we naturally require material objects to get by in life. In fact, we can classify material objects easily into *needs* and *wants.* We need food, water, and shelter to survive. We place our trust in the food we eat and the water we drink because we expect it to bring us health by quenching our immediate thirst and sating our hunger. Should we have an adverse reaction to something we ingest, we say, "I'm not eating that again." That object has lost our trust, and thus our loyalty recedes from that object. This holds true for tools that enable us to perform tasks more efficiently, as well. A soldier is loyal to their rifle as they know it will enable them to survive in a hostile environment. Truly, anything material/physical may fall into this category.

Values. Values stem from material objects. Values are exactly that: things that we place value on dependent on our loyalties to them. Humans naturally covet or hoard things that they desire more of. For some folks, they hoard wealth when others hoard food. I don't intend on these terms sounding negative, it is a part of human nature to want, own, and collect things. An avid cinematic enthusiast may collect movies and add them to her collection. A photographer by trade likely owns multiple cameras and multiple fixtures for that camera, on top of a plethora of camera-related equipment and attachments. Values give context to the objects that we place loyalty in, so we naturally gravitate to wanting/owning particular types of objects. This may also inform our perception of *material wealth.*

Principles. Principles align with spirituality, the human spirit. Principles are to personal aspirations as Values are to objects. The subject matter of principles lies within the ethereal plane of human thought. Honor, dedication, motivation, innovation, truly a slough of workplace motivational portraits could fit here in the realm of principles. These are characteristics that we value among ourselves and others. This is where religion most aptly fits into the role of morals: religions and spirituality help guide our personalities to develop, grow, and learn in certain ways. Now, we can start to see that loyalty in such ideals can start bringing people together. When it comes to human social psychology, like typically attracts like and we see folks congregating with similar principles on particular days of the week, on sanctioned holidays, and joining each other based not on their loyalty to one another, but their conjoined loyalty as presented to each other for a common set of principles.

People. Our classic conception of loyalty rests within the notion that we're loyal to other people. As a species, we naturally gravitate towards those who are like us. From a social psychology standpoint, we are most typically attracted to people who look like us, think like us, behave like us, and feel emotions like us. We need other humans to foster cognitive, behavioral, and emotional interdependence in order to feel attraction. These dependencies help us feel connected to the ones we love most: friends, family, and romantic partners. It's no coincidence, then, that these are the people we trust the most. Familiarity with others, familiarity with objects and concepts too, keep our loyalties tethered to people we most trust or are most familiar with.

Analyzing people and our interactions brings us to my definition of *moral authority*: *Power granted principally by the construction of loyalty.* This notion of loyalty allows a complete deconstruction and analysis of our personal relationships. It prefaces loyalty as a social construct. It allows us to ask ourselves, "Who am I loyal to and why? Why do I trust them and why do I have these interactions? What do I owe these folks? Do we owe anything to anyone, to anything?" This self-analysis enables one to self-criticize, learn, and understand oneself and one's interests at a fundamentally intimate level. This analysis may sound cynical, in fact it may sound purposely manipulative. I posit these thoughts chiefly as a foundation for more content I wish to talk on another time: *purpose* – what drives us and why? Personally, I don't believe that we owe anything to anyone, however, without caring for others genuinely and forging strong bonds based in moral authority, I would fail to cultivate feelings of worthiness and meaning. Others might be different, but without other people, existence would simply be meaningless long-term. *There would be no survival of species, only survival of self, ending in extinction.* The study of psychology would be a much more fitting pursuit to investigate this particular sub-topic further.

Organizations / Brotherhoods. Organization transcends the ties shared with one other person when we initiate trust among a broader range of people. This will logically follow as you meet new people, involve yourself in new environments, and work for a living. Your ties to people and places that you attend with a sense of duty will begin to foster conscious and unconscious loyalties to the organization that surrounds that particular environment. This may be the earliest point within our framework that *leadership* may be applied and understood. Defining leadership would be a futile effort here considering the wide array of definitions ascribed to "leadership" from the common human to the most remarkable of us. I will not define leadership here, but we can certainly declare that a leader *commands* loyalty in their particular environment. A leader does not command respect, but it can be earned through an exhibition of mutual trust. The leader who is loyal to their mission and provides for their subordinates to accomplish their collective goal will earn trust from those subordinates and they will grow ever loyal. When the implicit contract of trust is broken, either the subordinates lose trust in the leader, or the subordinate receives administrative punishment as decreed by the organizations they fall within (depending on which party broke their trust).

Organizations form due in part by the coagulation of several people's trust in one or few people. Leaders naturally arise when necessity of survival demands it. Recall *loyalty* – rooted in trust and conducive to survival. The trust in one person as granted by the loyalties of the many is a testament to that one person's tact, resourcefulness, wisdom, skill, strength, and many more qualities that the one may exhibit. In one way or many, the traits of the leader enable the subordinate to *survive* for better, worse, or meeting the status quo. A leader may fail to provide for their subordinates, and those subordinates may not have alternatives to trust in. When trust breaks down in an isolated environment, those who are most skillful or physically strong might easily assume command over their former superior. Hence, cultivating trust is a leader's primary responsibility in any organization and misuse of loyalties should be avoided and discouraged to the maximum extent.

RECAP ON TRIBAL MORALS

Denoting these objects of loyalties as *Tribal Morals* seems to be conducive to studying how human beings first began socializing and growing beyond small units of hunter-gatherers. I will attempt to posit a working definition now subject to future criticism and revision:

Tribal Morals – comprehensive set of logic that helps us determine what we need to survive by trusting our internal and others' external behavioral patterns within our most familiar environments

I'll quickly posit two more definitions, ones that likely have psychological definitions by another name:

Internal Behavioral Patterns – our personal thoughts and feelings that inform conscious and unconscious decisions

External Behavioral Patterns – experiences with our environments outside of our mind that inform our conscious and unconscious decisions through stimuli

It's extremely important to note that I've broadly defined every type of experience that humans may encounter by lumping them into *internal experiences* of the mind and *external experiences* that *affect* the mind and the body. These contextualize the raw inputs of everyday life that help us determine how we're going to survive in the short term. The act of experiencing something forces us to rationalize and perceive a particular thing in a particular way. Once our perceptions rationalize a positive or negative reaction, we choose whether to trust the information attained from that experience. Trust can be assessed in two ways: one can trust that an external behavioral pattern is beneficial or they may trust that something is malignant. I struggle using the term "distrust" if only for the logical reasoning that if you distrust something, it's because you trust that it will be disadvantageous to you.

Tribal Morals serve one foundational purpose: they help us survive. The definition of Tribal Morals intentionally echo that of Loyalty. I would argue that these five items under the umbrella of Tribal Morals are necessary for any person's long-term survival, just as Loyalty is necessary for survival for any amount of time. Tribal Morals identify who our "inner circles" are. They help us realize what is important to us at our individual cores. These morals form the basis of higher-ordered society by laying a foundation for human behavior in social and nonsocial contexts.

Loyalties are blind to the concept of "right" and "wrong." *Loyalty places trust in the things that enable survival.* If a crime lord subsists off their illicit gains and commands respect from their subordinates, then they are committing to a way of life and pattern of behavior that enables them and others to survive. Loyalties to this organization remain firm so long as the subordinates remain content with their conditions and their leaders remain committed to their purposes. People aligned to such an organization would view "right" as committing crimes, while others would view such actions disdainfully and call for their imprisonment to end the behavior which they see being disadvantageous to their survival.

THE COMMUNAL MORALS

Community. "A sense of community," the "community around you." What do these mean? In our graphic, Community holds a special spot as the transition between Communal Morals and Tribal Morals. It is also the last direct link to the fundamental ideas of Loyalty. It's understandable that one may feel entitled to hold a place within their community or that one may feel obligated to their community. Imagine going to the local barber shop or salon and catching up on the news, talking with the hairstylists and learning about their fire fighter husbands and talking about how they should raise their kids in a different school system.

Community – we can observe two ideas implicit in the etymology of the word: *Comm-* and *unity.* One might rationally gather that this simply means "common unity," or "shared unity." These interactions we have with people in our day to day lives, the physical locations we spend time at, the young grocery store workers that you talk to whenever you go through the self-checkout line (Yes Reid, I'm talking about you) all foster this common sense that we're in this world living life together. *Common Sense.* I'm not using that in the colloquial fashion but rather to mean *shared sense*. Perhaps this may be where we see roots in empathy and sympathy.

Nonetheless, a community is a coalition of people spanning different brotherhoods and creeds while retaining the capability to function loosely as one unit. Communities come together to watch their children play sports. Communities rally around other loyal community members in need. Again, this is why Loyalty remains key: should a community member shirk the values of their greater community, become a criminal, or otherwise cause harm to others, they lose their moral grasp on their community members and may cascade down a path of irreverence and isolation. A disloyal member of the community is undeserving of aid or support, so those disloyal members seek loyalty in other rejects to find tribally important matters to them and begin fostering new communities.

Resources / Commodities. It may very well be stated that each higher echelon in the spiral is a critical step. It is important to note that each step up from here represents a significant increase in the magnitude of capability that humans possess. Resources and commodities present a huge leap forward in human thought and prioritization for the sake of survival. Resources simply represent all the materials that a community values to ensure operations of the greater society. Notice that they're placed above *Material Objects* in our graphic. Given that we have a functional community, the people within a community will seek resources to gather in order to maintain their way of life.

Primitively speaking, we can envision a trade and barter system evolving from the acquisition of resources and commodities. Imagine a feudal or colonial society. A wood cutter might provide wood for a carpenter. A carpenter might provide shelter to the chef, the smith, and the doctor. The chef will provide food for the many, with ingredients gathered by the herbalist, farmer, and hunter. The smith will provide tools for the wood cutter, the doctor, and in turn the doctor would ensure health to their community. By prioritizing roles and resource acquisition within a community, survival needs may be distributed among members to ease the collective burden on any one individual attempting to acquire all of these skills. This allows people to cultivate expertise, enabling foundations of knowledge to be conceived and passed between members and generations. Knowledge, then, may be viewed as a resource that communities try to cultivate and exploit in order to survive and thrive.

Economy. A novel step up from Resources/Commodities, Economy is merely the effective management of resources and proper evaluation of resources after being acquired. Economies in society are like arteries within the body. Communities are the organs and resources are the blood. Economies are concerned with the efficiency and logistics of transaction management between people. Currency, or a valued medium to conduct trade with, may be used as a placeholder for goods and services. In fact, currency allows for communities to trade truly any good for any service. A trade and barter system effectively breaks down in a modern society when you can picture yourself at a restaurant. The server asks, "do you have medicine for my dying child? If not, you're not getting served and I'm serving someone who can help me."

Economy allows a flow of services to goods, goods to services, goods to goods, and services to services. A luxury such as a restaurant would fail to work should there not be a medium with which to handle all transactions with. While there exist several forms of currency within the world, mapping the value of one currency to another is a trivial task, just as converting from empirical to metric units is for measurement. Everything and every skill has inherent value, and economies breathe life into an otherwise stagnant system where communities fail to broaden their horizons or capabilities. Utilizing economies, we are capable of contextualizing a need for any material, any service, and shaping societies to include all people in all walks of life because we all add value to our community in some way, shape, or form. Economy capitalizes on that total value of community – human and material capital.

Standard of Living / Livelihood. Now that we have an established method for acquiring goods and utilizing services, we can improve our standard of living and our livelihood efficiently. This Communal Moral idea founds itself in both Values and Principles, suggesting that with sufficient resources and availability of resources to enable thriving lives, community members may search for items, associations, equipment, among many other things that improve the health and quality of one's existence. Utilizing their economies as rational utility maximizers, we might expect that people pursue walks of life to remain healthy, educated, and constantly striving to improve and succeed more. Now, behavioral economics would tell us this is NOT how human beings act, and this should be taken into consideration. With the resources and opportunities seemingly abundant in their environment, what barriers prevent people from maximizing their utility and improving their quality of life? How can we analyze behavioral economics to better understand how people carve their lives out within their environments? Note: I use *environment* as a broader term than *Community*, simply because their environment now includes socioeconomic and personal predispositions to determine how someone behaves in a societal context. How people maximize their participation in economy will determine their behavior and their quality of life.

Culture. Culture is the culmination of interaction within a community. Culture roots the foundation of a community and fosters *identity*. Culture is broader than one community, it transcends multiple layers of identity that invoke a great recognition of diversity within the scope and scale of a particular environment. For example, I am an American, Ohioan, Clevelander, Buckeye, Amazonian, young, adult male. There are several other identities that I find agency in, however, this gets the ideas of Culture across at face value and the forms which Culture takes. The intermixing of all these facts and my context within society based on these facts adds diversity to my community and environment, which enriches the culture around me if the community is accepting of my agency according to the various ways I assume identity.

Culture is extremely hard to pin down. To restate the above example, there can exist culture and identity in several different levels of societal structure. There exists an *American culture, an Ohioan culture, a Columbus culture, an OSU culture...* One can nitpick and analyze cultures and subcultures all day long, but what matters here is the metastructure of what culture *is*. Does Culture *qua*

Culture exist, or is it merely a fabrication of human spirit that allows us to heuristically associate with others we consider similar to ourselves?

Culture may be the first (and only) idea in the Spiral of Loyalty that I consider *hyper-permeable.* There may exist a culture between any one person with any other number of people. Cultural identity transcends the self and the community, permeating the barriers between every type of human being, hence the term *hyper-permeable/permeability.* There exists a very real difference in culture between the farmer and the business person. Despite this clear and immense difference, they may share values and principles exemplified within their own communities that help connect people in all the same or similar fashions as each other, hence they are culturally connected. Perhaps they witness an attack on their mutual identity and share the same resolve to defend their cultural cohort. Perhaps it's as simple as sharing the identity of being human and relating to each other on that basis alone that instills culture, permits growth, and inculcates communal identity. Culture is a fundamental building block to higher forms of society, and ambitious in nature. The ambition to foster ever broader cultural identities and include broader swathes of society suggest Culture's place in between Communal and Visionary Morals. Again, Culture is the culmination of interaction within a community and the building block to envision higher forms of society.

RECAP ON COMMUNAL MORALS

If Tribal Morals are a set of logic emanating from the self and experience to make choices, then *Communal Morals* are a set of logic applied to a group of people to make choices based on the members, values, and principles of your community. In the same spirit as *Tribal Morals,* we will craft another definition subject to evaluation:

Communal Morals – comprehensive set of logic with foundations in the construction of Tribal Morals that enable us to trust our communities and collectively improve our chances of survival.

One more:

Communal Behavioral Patterns – the collective thoughts

and feelings of a community that inform decisions within communities and guide interaction with other communities.

Cohesion presents itself as a salient idea throughout this discussion. Humans need to act cohesively as one body in order to survive better and improve conditions. Without a distribution of labor or a prioritization of work, humans would undoubtedly be over-tasked to provide for themselves, let alone cohabitate or have a family. Communities provide a loose framework for collaborations and transactions to occur to increase the output of their community and also maximize utility. A single parent of an infant must still work, and if their community fails to provide support in nannying/daycare services, they will struggle to provide for their child or work enough to get by. However, if there's an established medium to trade childcare for resources, then this burden is lifted and every party benefits.

It's clear in the above example how Communal Morals are exemplified, but how does one identify a Communal Behavioral Pattern? These behavioral patterns may be easiest to conceive by envisioning the culture of a community. What do people in your community do most often? How do we interact with each other? The communal behavioral patterns of being an Ohio State student may include watching the football games, eating at dining halls, crawling up and down high street every Friday through Sunday night. These behavioral patterns shape identity in a hyper-permeable fashion. People who are exposed to this culture may be enticed to partake in it. People who emulate this culture are prone to spread these ideas implicitly or explicitly, influencing those around them. People who reject these behavioral patterns remain largely unaffected. Friction between cultural groups who behave according to different principles opens the door to conflict and conflict resolution: learning opportunities abound in this frictional space, assuming a posture to change either culture's communal behavioral patterns, whether that's through growth or destruction.

Culture presents immense complexities to the framework of the Spiral of Loyalty. Despite its hyper-permeability, it serves as a rigid transitionary step between communities and higher echelons of moral order. Communities will largely remain loyal to their salient cultural groups and attempt to increase the efficacy of their programs and tools that enable people to live happily together. Culture begets culture, and the rise of broader/narrower identities is inevitable.

Metastructure, Substructure, and Hyper-permeability. I feel extremely compelled to describe these effectively. Let's try to prescribe a definition to these:

> *Hyper-permeability – the notion that any idea, skill, art, craft, or interaction between human beings in general has the propensity to duplicate ad infinitum through emulation and mimicking of other human beings.*

> *Metastructure – the underlying human infrastructure enabling understanding and connection between all unique identifiable cultures within a particular environment which combine salient cultures into one or few broad, identifiable groups.*

> *Substructure – the underlying human infrastructure enabling understanding and connection between*

members of a culture within a particular environment which fracture salient cultures into smaller, more numerous groups.

I am satisfied with these terms. *Hyper-permeability* proffers the idea that any *single* culture may transmit between cultures and cultural groups. *Metastructure* proffers the idea that each unique culture networks with other cultures in order to construct broader cultural identities. *Substructure* proffers the idea that members of one cultural identity may own multiple identities within their shared cultural space. We might now look at cultures and communities with a "yard stick." The community of Ohio State University combines many unique cultural and ethnic groups under the identity of "Buckeye." The *substructure* of Ohio State may reveal clubs, programs, different colleges and age groups, and so on whose members share affiliation and cultivate identity. The *metastructure* of Ohio State is that of universities and schools across Ohio and the US; it forms a part of the city of Columbus and the affiliates of Ohio State enjoy the amenities provided by the city. The identity of "Buckeye" is *hyper-permeable:*

people in and around Columbus, even inside and outside Ohio in general, praise the university, sports teams, and culture. They duplicate this culture through emulation of these ideas both consciously and unconsciously through words and actions, even if they share no direct affiliation.

I feel that these definitions are profound, yet, we're only halfway done describing the Spiral of Loyalty to its known boundaries. The fluidity of the substructure and metastructure might very well be applied to Economies and Brotherhoods/Organizations. Culture and its hyper-permeable nature may very well be applicable to nearly every type of human interaction. Notice its position above "People" within the Spiral. As with people, further investigation may suggest studies into psychology, cultural anthropology, and history to gain better understanding of how we interact with each other in societies.

VISIONARY MORALS

A Preface. I dub "Visionary Morals" as such due to their incredibly unstable and ambitious nature. I will refrain from crafting a definition until further investigation, just as with the other morals. How are the Visionary Morals unstable? How do we rise above the hyper-permeable principle of Culture? What more order can we derive from human interaction? Following the blatant logic of the Spiral thus far, we can see that the next logical step from Culture would be forming Governments. Naturally, cultures combining with each other cause friction between their constituent members and fosters an inherently unstable environment. Though mixing cultures can lead to conflict and conflict resolution, the relative polarity of these groups' principles will determine how ordered their long-term peace will be. With these notions posited, we will begin our investigation into governments.

Governments. Let's begin by analyzing our own government. What do we see? Let's start from a level of increasing exposure in our daily lives. Bottom up, Government presents itself locally, regionally (state), and federally. It's immediately apparent that there exists an inherent metastructure in our Government constructions alone. Our local governments interact with other communities and cities on a daily basis to ensure that mutually beneficial relationships are cultivated and each locality's residents are benefitting from their partnership. Our state governments help local governments survive by providing county offices representing the state. These offices permit residents, agencies, businesses, and multiple other types of organizations to contact the state for resources and aid. The State yields resources to residents in good standing, and those in good standing with the government may be coerced to follow certain regulations lest their good standing be revoked (laws). This follows from regional authorities to the federal authorities, that States may request federal assistance to further assist their constituents. The federal government yields resources so long as those States are properly coerced to follow laws and regulations to remain in good standing with the National leadership. What are these levels of Government achieving in this structure? How do these relate to cultural goals and constructions?

Governments act as a way to consolidate cultural goals and prioritize objectives for the *greater good* of all involved, affected by, or otherwise subordinate to a particular cultural group. By "greater good," I mean "that which improves the quality of life for the most amount of people possible." Inevitably, constituents of different cultures within governments will be dissatisfied with some results of higher-order decision making and compromising. This should be expected invariably, with measures in place to adequately manage the expectations of constituent cultures to assuage friction and remedy any aggression onset by decisions of higher leaders. Governments do NOT achieve goals for themselves, they achieve goals for their constituents. A government without constituents is nothing more than an organization of figureheads lacking any credible, legitimate authority.

It is important to note that the greater good cannot be manipulated based on class. Infinitely improving the life of one person will not balance out and increase the welfare of the greater good while others suffer. Rather, we would have to prescribe some form of measurement to analyze how well people are doing. This may simply look like meeting basic needs and assigning a value to each of those needs as they're met/sustained. This will prove to be the grounds for an interesting study in the future, if values can be weighted, measured, and objectified. If one class identifiable in society was improved to the detriment of others, we might verily say that quality of life is not improving for the most amount of people.

Leaders in governments are effectively cultural leaders from their localities/regions. These cultural representatives convene to boil down their separate issues into one primary agenda that can be used to address each constituencies' issues most efficiently. Properly motivated Governments mitigate the threat of improper distribution of resources which may cause conflict by developing appropriation plans and utilizing logistics to ensure healthy flows of wants and needs to their affiliated cultural groups. A Government manages economies and people with varying interests, a tough balancing act that increases in difficulty as we move outward in the Spiral.

Governments are the first synthetic moral construction beyond that of typical human nature, I'd argue. A government coalesces to allow the cooperation of tribes, communities, cultures, economies, a great many things we have discussed already. Cultures might truly be the highest order of natural construction, seeing that a culture will form in about any environment imaginable. A workplace culture will form just as a community culture will form just an institutional culture will form. But governments do not form from nothing. Government does not happen naturally. To relate to Plato's Allegory of the Cave, it has taken great strength, resolve, and practice to steer away from tribal and primitive norms to create what we now know as society today. It could be endlessly speculated why the first tribes began working together, but should we continue to fail to work together and stay separate, we may very well begin to regress. Governments are the first Visionary Moral because they're the first step beyond what we know as natural and enable humans to enhance all aspects of their daily life and the lives of their future generations.

Nations. A Nation might simply be understood as a coalition of smaller governments. A Nation may be the identity that a governmental structure has given its people. A Nation may be a sovereignty that differs from that which you know. Let's chase this idea: a nation is a broad cultural identity ascribed to people and territory recognized as subordinate to a particular government. It's a cultural identity that specifically includes multiple cultures. A Nation *qua* Nation achieves collaborative goals of multiple cultures living together. While government is concerned with *governance*, Nations are concerned with *claim*.

Two ideas contextualize this assertion. Governments provide oversight and infrastructure. As described before, they convene to meet the needs of their constituents through interaction and deliberation. Nations *claim* all that is beneath them. The first idea, *borders,* is a territorial claim that subjects all those within the borders to cultures and customs conducive to fostering national identity. That same Nation claims its people with citizenship, some countries call it a "birthright." Nations effectively limit the goodness potential of a government by taking ownership over their subordinate realm and crafting exclusionary measures to keep others out. Governments are concerned with connection, nations are concerned with control, which leads to a natural tension when considering domestic and international interests.

This concept is not so easy to grasp. Perhaps it'd be easier if we claimed, "I have a sense of national pride, I don't feel involved in government." This would be a view largely held by many Americans. Government necessarily takes care of the details in society in an effort to make living much easier for all those subordinate within a nation's territory and citizenry. The national identity is much more organic in its construction. A Nation might recoil from the shock of a tragedy or it may rejoice by celebrating a momentous achievement. Reactions from an informed nation will be immediate while government organizes for action in the shadows. Nations provide a societal, physical, and informational context to prime peoples' minds for multifarious service of their nation as a citizen and defender of collective national agendas and values.

Cultivation. With an established network of leadership infrastructure and an established identity spanning broad swathes of land and diverse cultures, we've defined what we might call a *national interest.* Goals pertaining to the national interest are conducive to the growth and *survival* of their populace. By remaining loyal (specifically, government leaders) to topics of national interest and public matters, we can *cultivate* our society to support our interests at home and abroad. Sometimes, our interests at home necessitate involvement of other entities, thus we also need to cultivate relationships on broader and more diplomatic scales. Just like cultures come together in a community, nations must work together to efficiently cultivate both human and economic capital to enable their long-term survival.

We enable Cultivation in many ways, but what distinguishes this as a Visionary Moral is the level of coordination necessary to efficiently and effectively sustain any form of long-term operation (strategy). This might be farming, this could be manufacturing, this could be diplomacy. To push even broader, we can think of cultivation as the resources necessary to enable the four instruments of national power: diplomatic, informational, military, and economic (DIME). Cultivation with regards to each of these instruments is almost absolutely necessary in today's world. A nation must cultivate diplomatic relationships to gain access to more resources (economic), but they must also cultivate their human capital using their available information systems (education) to produce more information (intelligence) to accomplish national goals. Military is a tool that utilizes production from the other three instruments in order to cultivate a high degree of human capital (skills, leadership) that may be used to conquer, defend, support, or deter other actors to keep them from interfering with our cultivation of resources.

The DIME instruments illustrate what Cultivation effectively produces and emphasizes a nation's ability to regulate their environment on a strategic scale. Naturally, any nation wants to be the strongest nation in all four DIME categories. Friction at the strategic level is understandably frightening to some. The same powers that can aid, support, and encourage growth across borders are the same powers that can choke, restrict, and destroy others. To what degree are the biggest and strongest nations obligated to help the weaker nations? Morality seems to deteriorate at the strategic operation of international affairs as governments quarrel with what their national interests should include and how to manipulate national identity to justify their actions. What is the barrier preventing unhindered cooperation between nations? What national interests are so important to necessitate strangleholds on other nations? Why must some international deals be carried out in secret? Do we really need a credible threat to keep society from deteriorating and motivate us to keep production and cultivation intact?

Provision / Protection. This is the final Visionary Moral, and naturally Provision/Protection are the accomplishments/products of the DIME instruments. What does the cultivation of DIME yield? Cultivating economy yields more resources, jobs, and enables the relevant governments to utilize these resources and *provide* for their peoples. Cultivating information yields higher levels of education, cultural awareness, and human capital conducive to achieving strategic goals. Cultivating military yields *protections,* which deter potential enemies and fight to protect both national interests and interests of the people. "Military" at the local level may resemble police forces, and in extremely rural areas, this could resemble a small organization of neighbors who vow to protect each other. Cultivating diplomacy yields greater access to more resources, broader *protections* due to acquiring allies interested in protecting resources for their benefit, and the ability to reinforce informational power by learning about more cultures and using their knowledge to mutually reinforce information between these allies.

What exemplifies "visionary" more than the Framers of the US Constitution? Provision/Protection are to morals as the Preamble is to the Constitution: both outline comprehensive goals solely dedicated to the people of [The United States]. The Preamble describes each visionary moral as we've defined: government ("to form a more perfect Union", invoking *governance*), nations ("secure the Blessings of Liberty to ourselves and our Posterity", invoking *claim*), cultivation ("insure domestic tranquility", "promote the general welfare," cultivating DIME), and Provision/Protection ("provide *for* the common defence", "Ordain and Establish this Constitution *for* the United States of America," emphasis on *for*).

The identification of goals at the strategic/visionary level helps inculcate identity that can be felt and admired within and outside of a nation's borders. To paraphrase my friend Luis, "I fled Venezuela because I feared for my life. Even though people talk about all these problems within the US, I still believe this is the best country in the world." Luis still experiences issues within the US, but despite this, he doesn't have to fear for his life, and he may begin rebuilding his loyalties from tribal morals on up as the US government provides the tools for his success and the innate protection he needs to keep surviving. I've also had the pleasure of meeting folks who've won the "Green Card Lottery," indicating there exist peoples abroad who will submit for even a chance to move to the US in hopes of cultivating a better future for themselves. This is the power of Provisions/Protections – these morals attract people who value the benefits of sound moral structure. (Note: "Establish Justice" was intentionally left out of the connection to the Preamble. This will be addressed.)

RECAP ON VISIONARY MORALS

In the beginning, we identified Visionary Morals as "incredibly unstable in nature." Despite the above arguments which may sound like stabilizing forces, there exists an underlying friction. As cultures coagulate and intermix, the glue that binds them will need occasional reapplication to keep these groups bound together. The might of one nation may be able to fracture another nation with one swift invasion. At the strategic level, situations are volatile, and it may seem like there are no "right" answers. Visionary Morals present a tough balancing act between different levels of strategic goals; attention to national interests may prevent attention from being spent on regional or local strategic interests. Using this information, let's try to craft a definition for Visionary Morals:

Visionary Morals – comprehensive set of logic synthetically constructed from Communal Morals that enable diverse populations across broad expanses to collaborate strategically to accomplish national and international societal objectives that enhance prospects for survival

I'm content with this definition, so long as one recalls *metastructure* and *substructure*. The thought of "nations" may produce images of countries and continents. Yet, it is extremely important to recognize that this Spiral flexes with scope and scale. A "nation" may indicate a city or a state, and we typically refer to connections between similarly situated localities as "interstate" or "intercity". A state, then, necessarily is a substructurally constructed "nation" (wow that's a mouthful). A coalition of countries (NATO) might be understood as a metastructurally constructed "nation."

Perhaps "unstable" is a poor quality to attribute to Visionary Morals. Rather, we can contextualize Visionary Morals as "reactive," such as a chemical reaction. When we bring other cultures, economies, and qualities of living together we can expect friction. The most salient friction will inevitably include: "They're different from us", "Why don't we have what they have", and "We don't share similar values/principles." Visionary Morals supply a vehicle with which to attempt management of all salient interests and defuse any potential conflicts at a strategic level. While these may provide a method to manage salient interests, they do NOT include a way to explicitly resolve friction.

The relative reactivity of Visionary Morals also stems from the management of personal loyalties and deconflicting personal interests from the interests of a nation. I contend that *corruption* is a product of poor personal management of duties and interests. A corrupt official, politician, or authoritative figure becomes corrupt because they value their own Tribal Morals over the Visionary or Communal Morals that enabled them to attain their present status in authority. In fact, we might assert that *all* moral authority is rooted in that authority which is granted to those who emulate the most exalted of morals. However, we have to remember that morals are nebulous and relative to one's own disposition and personal loyalties. Moral exaltation to one may be moral condemnation to another. Thus, we may observe authority figures structuring their organizations expressly to include those with similar moral character, whether their morals exemplify loyalties to humanity or loyalty to themselves (or anything else, for that matter).

The notion of *strategy* has arisen here naturally as we discussed the implications of the instruments of national power. Some may argue that strategy would be included in earlier stages of the Spiral, though I would contend that implementing strategy would require a flexing of the Spiral to the appropriate substructure or metastructure. Strategy asserts that there is a broad goal, a greater plan. Governments hint that there exists a "greater good" to strive for relative to their own interests. Strategy is maximizing the positive outcome long-term to achieve an ultimate goal or set the pretext for an even broader goal. Due to the relative scope and scale of the Visionary Morals, we can observe how strategic decisions need to be considered to increase survival prospects for those residing in a particular nation.

We must lastly note that each Visionary Moral enables a higher degree of survival. By bringing communities together, we can avoid violent conflict and encourage mutually beneficial relationships. By working towards broad goals, we may increase qualities of living and enhance our economies to better provide for our smaller communities. By protecting our interests, we can assure our peoples that others will not take that which enables us to thrive. By cultivating all that we have access to, we can increase efficiency of outputs in terms of DIME instruments and improve the overall quality of society by allowing more resources to reach more locations. By laying claim to both people and territory, nations and governments can employ their human capital to exploit economic capital for strategic gains. We *trust* these constructions to enable our survival, that their continued operations allow us to enjoy our lives and thrive, compelling us to seek employment, pay taxes, and raise future generations loyal to our nations.

IDEAL MORALS

If Tribal Morals help the self survive, Communal Morals help others survive, and Visionary Morals help various societies survive, then Ideal Morals help *everyone* survive. They reserve the title of "Ideal" for the sole reason that they're incredibly difficult to strive for, let alone emulate perfectly. We can see the reactive friction of Visionary Morals in the independent constructions of different nations and governments. Not every culture, government, nation, or use of DIME powers is concerned with accomplishing goals while considering the scope of the negative impacts. A bomb dropped on a military target may achieve a strategic objective without consideration for the families of those killed to achieve it. Firing an employee may save an organization money, but doing so may harm that person's ability to provide for themselves and others. Ideal Morals aren't merely concerned with outcomes at face value – Ideal Morals are concerned with improving the consequences of consequences, an endless interdependent chain of actions where one objective improvement in one's life can affect all others, and so improvement of all lives should be pursued.

Equity. Equity naturally presents itself as the first Ideal Moral. Here, we return to the Preamble, invoking "Establish Justice." To posit the question that philosophers have asked for millennia: What is justice? What is fairness? Is this a question of due process or subjective opinion of relevant authority figures? Elsewhere, I dichotomize Aristotle's "Four Causes" to help distinguish that which is justified, and thus becoming of justice. For those familiar with the Four Causes, I posit the following interpretation:

1ˢᵗ Cause – Formal Cause
Aristotelian "substances" – Truth and Fallacy

2ⁿᵈ Cause – Material Cause
Matter and Form – Being and Non-Being

3rd Cause – Efficient Cause
The "Movement" or change – Time; Growth and Decay

4th Cause – Final Cause
*The End Goal – **Justice** and Injustice*

Let's return to the notion of Ideal Morals, that lives should be improved so that others, potentially all, may also be improved. We might view the objective *truth* of Ideal Morals to be that which improves the lives of others. We might identify the *matter* that is necessary to improve these lives, that the means of improvement actually exist and are plausible to provide. Then, as a function of *time*, if we reach an end that improves a life or lives that enables them to *grow*, we may assert that the end of our actions is *justified*, thus we've delivered a form of *justice*. I further assert that Equity embodies this application of justice according to my brief interpretation of Aristotle's Four Causes.

Equity goes further than a prompt and effective delivery of justice. Equity desires to achieve fairness. *Is one end justified relative to other similar sets of circumstances?*

Equity strives to ensure that justice is in fact justified. We can observe in our society initiatives that pursue equitable outcomes by writing into law the prohibition of behavior and actions that lead to impediments on others. Despite prohibiting active impediments by writing rules into law, inherent biases lasting from cultural differences/conflict limit the extent to which these laws are useful. People who are biased against others will knowingly or unknowingly commit injustices which lead to the worsening of circumstances and thus inequitable. Is the justice brought about by equity and equality laws justified? Yes, their intent is to improve the lives of those who experience injustice by attempting to eliminate the injustice.

It is apparent now just what Equity means within the context of Ideal Morals. Have we explored every way in which Equity is morally significant? No. We have prescribed a broad interpretation of Equity – *the justification of justice.* I'd like to emphasize that the impact of Equity directly ties into the treatment of people within one and across several cultures. A homogenized culture may very well have a high achievement of Equity within their immediate community. The metastructure which their culture is a part of may treat them differently based on the salience of their culture, their relevance to other cultures, or their importance of their placement within their metastructure. In the most extreme inequitable circumstances, this treatment may resemble genocide. In an equitable circumstance, we might envision a community with a food surplus to share with a community experiencing a food shortage. Such acts might be considered "humanitarian" and "ethical". It is certainly equitable in that it achieves an improvement in others' lives without unduly impinging the lives of others, and thus morally justified. How do we bridge the barrier that prevents Equity from full realization?

Assimilation. At a first glance, this may immediately resemble cultural assimilation, however, this is not my intention. A broadly homogenized culture, though perhaps equitable, would stagnate without diversity. The moral significance of Assimilation rests in the ability of other cultures to engender and accept differences. Assimilation is not merely providing ESL classes to help immigrants learn English, it is the provision of foreign language classes to their own citizens of the languages most prevalent in particular communities. Assimilation is shopping at Jungle Jim's, a superstore for food and products catering to a vast array of different cultural tastes.

Assimilation is an Ideal Moral because this would bridge the barrier encountered in achieving Equity. By accepting those across different cultures, backgrounds, ethnicities, and recognizing the fact that we are all human beings worthy of esteem and dignity we may begin to erode ingrained cultural norms and biases that pit people against each other. If governments can unite cultures, then the adhesive they need to use to effectively increase collaboration and produce improvement in all lives is Assimilation, a broad and comfortable acceptance of others.

This Ideal moral is overly optimistic. To achieve progress to a degree where even one person might accept a different culture, it may be necessary to reeducate that person entirely and deconstruct their view on their own reality. To achieve Assimilation, one must breakdown, reevaluate, and reconfigure their own Tribal Morals; most notably, they would have to reconfigure their loyalties to principles and people that they hold most dear. Their cultural beliefs would result from a communal like-mindedness, thus to completely reform one's loyalties to principles and peoples, they might effectively excommunicate themselves from the life that they know! This is to say that in the first place, one must be open-minded enough to even consider these other values. Thus, the hesitancy to assimilate evaluated from the perspective of one's own natural selfish desire to remain comfortable and thrive is completely understandable.

So, how do we begin to breakdown the barriers that prevent Assimilation? I will refer to what little I know about social psychology and my own experiences in molding workplace cultures over time. In social psychology, we are attracted to things and people that we are most familiar with and similarly unattracted to things and people we are unfamiliar with. It makes sense that we initially are uninterested or completely dismissive of other cultures. However, the closer these cultures are to each other, then over time, we might expect Assimilation to happen naturally, so long as the two cultures are not antagonistic towards one another. In the workplace, I've witnessed constant kind gestures result in the return of kind gestures. Providing support and aid even when it's not necessary, being loyal to others with no expectation of loyalty in return, will engender loyalty. Showing an interest in learning about someone else's culture by learning a few words in their native language may produce loyalty. By encouraging growth and producing loyalty in others, one may effectively accomplish an assimilative goal. One person doing this gains many friends; dozens of people doing this redefines their culture and community.

Indirect Governance. If governance is effectively how a government governs, then Indirect Governance implies a much more hands-off approach to governing people. At this point, the people are effectively in full control of what they do with little to no participation in government. Indirect Governance within this framework can really only be met once the antecedent morals have been achieved. In an environment where all peoples are accepting of one another, where Equity prevents the occurrence of discrimination by any means and provides opportunities to all, then we might have a robust society where no one subsists on their government for any direct support. If we can imagine a community where all are employed and needs are met, then we could imagine having to only pay taxes and deal with bureaucracy when dealing with substantial property purchases or life changes. Even then, envisioning a world of such unrealistic optimization might include the infrastructure to deal with such events within one's own powers, if we reach a point where all people could be trusted to accurately handle their personal administrative affairs.

For the most part, I envision myself as being a participant of Indirect Governance: I am employed, I pursue opportunities where they're available, and the most interaction I have with the government above me is usually paying a tax or visiting the BMV. These interactions are made simpler and more fluid with the constant innovation of technology and businesses which minimize interaction with bureaucracy as much as possible. In fact, I would bargain that the government above us would love to save costs by reducing government employment and seeing people competently manage their own affairs. It is not that simple, and the society we have constructed and participate in would require a total restructuring to accomplish such a feat. Either a society such as ours risks chaos and disorder by reforming all that we know, or the changes are made gradually over decades and centuries to allow for generational adaptation.

This might sound Utopian, and perhaps it is. However, I will contest that any of the Ideal Morals are nigh impossible to truly achieve, hence why they are "ideals" and not practicable. Do I think this is achievable? Certainly not in my lifetime, and maybe not even for centuries. I do hope humanity lasts long enough to collectively aspire to such an achievement. While Indirect Governance can be observed to some degree in societies today, it is not universal. The effectiveness of this moral, along with the other Ideal Morals, is contingent on it being universally observable and actionable. For Indirect Governance to be universally observable, it would require both Equity and Assimilation to be universally observable, and even when both Morals meet that condition, it would be a long time before those able-bodied and able-minded people in society are universally self-sufficient and can forget about Direct Governance tools to assist them.

What would governments do if they were not actively governing people? Well, it would allow governments to utilize revenues in ways that explicitly provide services for people. While the population may be administratively self-sufficient, they still need infrastructure, schools, leadership, protection, environmental regulation, power, water, transportation, and trade regulation to name a few salient government functions. While it is ideal that everyone at this point follows the law, some form of peacekeeping needs to be upheld to apprehend criminals. The prison system should be reformed at this point to effectively rehabilitate, reeducate, and reintroduce prisoners back into society equitably.

Moreover, if government employment could effectively be minimized, then revenues from taxation could also go to projects that not only benefit immediate society, but all society. This may look like disease research and prevention, space exploration and colonization, and distribution of surplus resources to regions that desperately need relief. The more governments that achieve a high level of

Indirect Governance could then collaborate and align to achieve these goals together, assimilating cultures, pooling resources, and sharing knowledge openly to encourage rapid technological innovation and growth. To apply social psychology to enormous proportions, if other countries see more advanced countries engaging in this behavior and being successful, then they too might emulate this behavior as time moves forward, mimicking what this success looks like. This leads to our final Ideal Moral.

Civilization. First, to use the Oxford Dictionary definition – the stage of human social and cultural development and organization that is considered most advanced.

Civilization is the highest Ideal Moral because it represents the culmination of all human achievement. Civilization represents the epitome of human ability and the ability of individual humans to achieve far more than was ever thought possible. Civilization is nonstop innovation that leads to achievements never before seen. If we can lead political, technological, and industrial revolutions, why not moral, philosophical, and behavioral revolutions too?

We undermine our own abilities to accomplish, achieve, and thrive by seeing barriers and immediately thinking: "Oh no, how much effort will this require? Is it really worth it? Maybe I'll just lead a life meeting the status quo. How hard do I have to try to be 'successful?'". The more I think about it, I think about how little effort is put into producing change in communities. Sure, a community may have its leaders and louder voices, but how many people listen? How does one inculcate change conducive to producing and emulating Ideal Morals?

One answer to achieving Civilization may be to emulate and practice the Ideal Morals constantly. Ensure that your justice is justified, and don't be afraid to make mistakes so long as you learn and fix them. Welcome others with open arms and an open mind. A smile and a wave to a stranger may feel odd, though it is a powerful gesture, in fact a welcome gesture most often. Help others become self-reliant, share your knowledge with them in hopes that they learn and grow. By emulating the very morals that we consider ideal, we may be able to cause a collective shift, a gradual shift in how the people around us think and operate. And what was that about

Ideal Morals? Ah yes, *consequences of consequences* – your act of kindness today may instill joy in someone, and that someone might return kindness to you or others as a result: an endless chain of consequences that results in the growth of potentially *all* human beings. Let's not forget, this works in reverse too: consequences of negativity may result in negativity, leading to an endless chain of decay in human thought and behavior.

Sure, this might all sound like an elaborate idealization of what we're capable of, that we can achieve a world holding hands and singing Kumbaya. I would challenge those cynics and critics of human behaviors and morals to identify all their loyalties according to the Spiral. I would imagine that of their loyalties, they can likely identify loyalties within Tribal and Communal Morals easily and plentifully. If they can identify an organization that they're a part of, then I'd challenge them to disconnect it and isolate it entirely from other entities. Even a principle that they're loyal to: if they cannot separate a principle expressly as their own, then it can be assumed that elsewhere in society that particular principle can be found emulated by others. While Tribal Morals are extremely intimate, they are difficult to separate from the morals that build upwards from the network of humanity's psyche. Even if our personal goals don't include idealized morals for all, our own set of morals produces loyalty to causes and goals broader than ourselves. This cannot be ignored. In fact, this aspiration to achieve might very well be the seat of all morals and loyalty. It is natural, then, that morals compound and aggregate into broadly impactful spectra that any human can relate to. Figure 2 below illustrates that these ideas are interconnected in a web of similarities, that each moral connected moving from outside-in contributes directly to the success/emulation of the inner morals and vice versa.

WRAP UP ON IDEAL MORALS

The Ideal Morals present plenty of concepts that need further exploration on their own. In fact, each topic discussed in this paper may be rightly deserving of its own analysis. What is important to note is both the ultimate impact of the morals and their relevant impact at present. We can't say that forms of Equity, Assimilation, Indirect

Governance, and Civilization don't exist. There are two important distinguishments that make Ideal Morals *Ideal:* that humans should strive to see that they're universally observable in all people and that they focus on improving the whole of the human existence.

> *Ideal Morals — comprehensive set of logic dedicated to the broad improvement of social, cultural, and economic conditions for all human beings through reproduction and emulation of such morals within Visionary, Communal, and Tribal Moral substructures.*

Wow, what the heck does that even mean? Well, as stated previously, the Spiral flexes and adjusts to the relevant substructures or metastructures. Thus, similar to Nations, we can flex Civilization to fit wholly within the context of a business, a team, a county, a state, a continent, or even your own neighborhood. Some of these might necessitate some vast extrapolations, but that is the beauty of this framework: we can fit it to any relevant structure, large or small, and then begin analyzing the substructural and metastructural components as needed.

To finish summarizing our definition of Ideal Morals, we can assert that emulation of Equity and Assimilation on small scales will see these reproduced on larger scales over time. This follows for Indirect Governance and Civilization, but the success of these two Ideal Morals are largely predicated on the broad adoption of the previous two to be emulated. By aspiring to achieve these ourselves and inspiring resolve in others to emulate these morals as conducive to the improvement of the lives of others, we might witness a moral revolution – I'd argue, a revolution much needed and well-overdue.

MORALS: WHAT ARE THEY?

In exploration of this framework, we have discerned that morals are largely used as a survival mechanism. Asserted earlier, *moral authority* is power granted principally by the construction of Loyalty. Loyalty is rooted in trust and conducive to survival. In order for any of these morals to work, there is a necessary level of trust, and the subject in receipt of trust prescribes a relationship of loyalty. Loyalties can be controlled, subverted, and otherwise manipulated to exert power over the Loyal. Loyalties hold so long as the prospect of survival remains intact. Thus:

Morals – sets of logic unique to single individuals which inform one's ability to establish trust in survival mechanisms in order to meet survival needs and thrive.

This definition fits with all sets of Tribal, Communal, Visionary, and Ideal Morals that came before. Utilizing the same principles of substructure and metastructure, we can broadly interpret an *individual* to mean a single person, a single community, a single nation, a single civilization. Each set of morals concerns themselves with survival of its current echelon, and is interrelated to all other moral constructions. Each set of morals builds off of itself and others to inspire an ultimate goal of globally recognized human companionship, dignity, and aspiration.

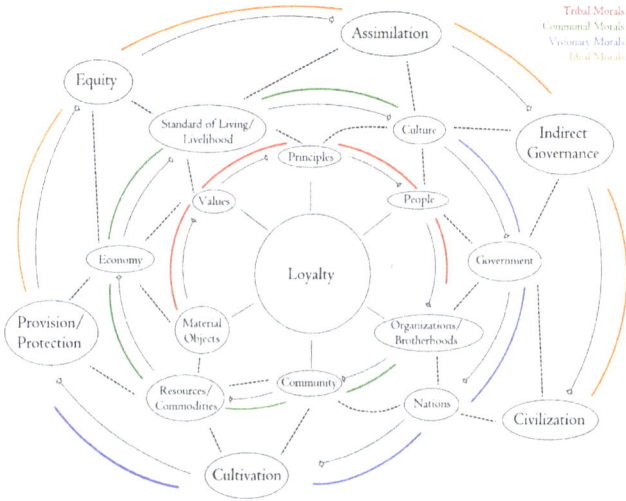

Figure 2: The Spiral of Loyalty illustrating interconnection of layered morals

Conclusion

The purpose of this paper was to inspire thought, solicit criticism, and investigate what these topics mean. In doing so, I discovered much, but I have more to gain from critics of these ideas. If you've read this, not only do

I thank you for your time, but I'd also like to solicit heavy feedback, as I will likely carry these values with me into my future and leadership philosophies.

The largest barrier to accomplishing any of these goals, in my humble opinion, are people who say "that's unrealistic, that's not possible." They're right: these ideas aren't possible to achieve when people aren't willing to initiate change in their immediate vicinities, let alone any form of metastructure/substructure. Whether it's sharing a laugh with a stranger at the grocery store, sweeping the trash out of your apartment's walkway, or telling an irate coworker "If you need anything, let me know. I'm here for you," you can make a small difference that will inspire a personal connection with Reid at the grocery store, it'll inspire your neighbor Julio to give you a light bulb that'll fit your porch light, and by thanking Lorenzo for his hard work, he will apologize for trying to start a fight and give you a list of beer recommendations. Perhaps general kindness was omitted from this paper, or maybe kindness is resultant from generally trusting humans. Regardless of circumstance, humans will support each other and moral support spontaneously generates from the loyalties we instill and inspire. Trusting each other is the key to progress; progress will improve lives, and suddenly idealized morals aren't so far away.

ABOUT THE AUTHOR

I'd consider my enthusiasm for writing one of my greatest strengths. For the past 3 years, I've journaled both in writing and in video formats, all done for the sake of self-reflection. This year, while attending Army ROTC training while pursuing a Master's degree and working my first full-time salary night job, I decided I somehow had enough time to write this short book.

One principle I live with is this: life is meaningless without others in it. Ultimately, we owe it to our fellow humans to work together to survive in the best ways we can. There's very little that we can't accomplish when we put our imaginations and efforts together.

I share my thoughts for the sole purpose that this book can spur thought among the readers in a positive, secular way. I intend to write more about Morals, Ethics, and Laws in due time as I pursue more education and experience. One thing I've learned in my short 25 years alive is that the price of education is only limited by your willingness to purchase a text-book and putting in the effort to read it. Find something that truly inspires you, and your thirst for knowledge will drive you to accomplish things you thought were never possible before.